Magical Beauties

Book 2

by

Cristina McAllister

Gypsy Mystery Arts

Magical Beauties Coloring Book; Book 2

This book is the second book in the "Magical Beauties" Coloring Book series by Cristina McAllister.

Copyright © 2017 Cristina McAllister
All rights reserved

Purchasers of this book may scan or copy and print pages for their own personal coloring use only, but cannot distribute, post online or sell them in any way. You may post *colored* pages on social media, if accompanied by an artist's credit and the book's title

Special Thanks to the members of the Cristina McAllister Coloring Club on Facebook. You all inspire me every day to keep making cool images so I can see how you bring them to li
:D

Published by Gypsy Mystery Arts
http://www.GypsyMystery.com

ISBN-13: 978-1977669711

ISBN-10: 1977669719

A Few Words From the Artist

Magical Beauties Book 1 has been my best-selling coloring book so far, and I've been delighted by the diverse ways that each colorist brings their own unique personality and vision to the images.

I hope Book 2 continues to inspire your creativity!

My goal for the artwork in this book was to create images that aren't terribly difficult to color but result in impressive finished pages. All it takes is a few basic coloring skills to make these pages shine, and my hope is that coloring these pages will help you hone those skills.

There are several design elements in these pages that can facilitate this:

* Mandala-like Elements and Patterns: elaborate adornments and decorative details are often created with simple shapes, abstract patterns and repeating elements that offer plenty of opportunities to create interesting color patterns and an endless variety of color schemes.

* Grayscale: While these pictures are not photorealistic 3D grayscale images, I have used some gray areas to indicate depth, dimension and dramatic lighting and also to clarify the images in some cases. The grays generally indicate where shadows fall, and you can use these tonal hints as guides to add some dimensional shading. Be sure to read the Coloring Tips section for instructions on how to make the most of the gray areas.

* Interesting Shapes: Some elements are as basic as you can get - simple circles or triangles, but I've tried to arrange them in interesting ways and also include a lot of intricate, organic shapes that wrap around other shapes. I find flowing my color into these kinds of shapes to be quite enjoyable.

* Engaging Characters: these magical beauties each have their own unique personality, look and mood. My hope is that they will inspire you to imagine your own unique character details. What kind of person is she? What are her powers? Her role in society? Her history? All of these are open for interpretation and I invite you to develop the characters, make them your own, and try using color to express those qualities.

If you are on Facebook, I invite you to join the Cristina McAllister Coloring Club to check out our inspiring collection of colored pages from my books and Share your own WIPs and finished pages.

If you enjoy this book, please take a few moments to post a review on the Amazon.com listing page. Those reviews really do make a difference to self-publishers and indie artists. Your feedback and support are invaluable!

Yours, *C. McAllister*

Cristina McAllister

Coloring Tips

How to Use Grayscale Areas to Create Dimension

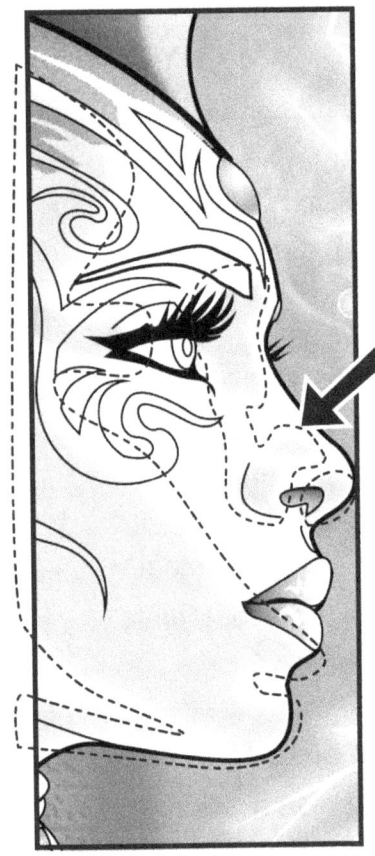

Gray areas indicate where shading can be used to create a sense of depth and dimension. Make note of where these gray areas are before you start coloring.

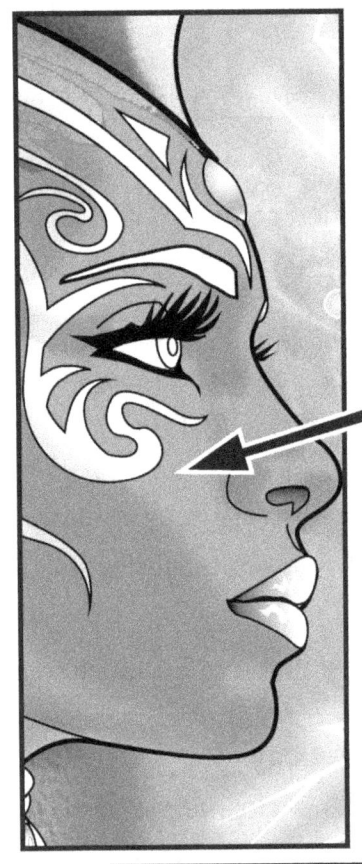

Fill in all skin-colored areas with a base fleshtone. ***Color over the gray areas as well as the white areas.*** You may have to use a bit more pressure with colored pencils in the gray areas. Even if you can barely see the color in darker areas, you want to tint the gray areas with color.

Using transparent colors works best, because the gray will show through. You can use the **Grayscale Test Sheet** at the back of this book to see how your colors look over gray areas.

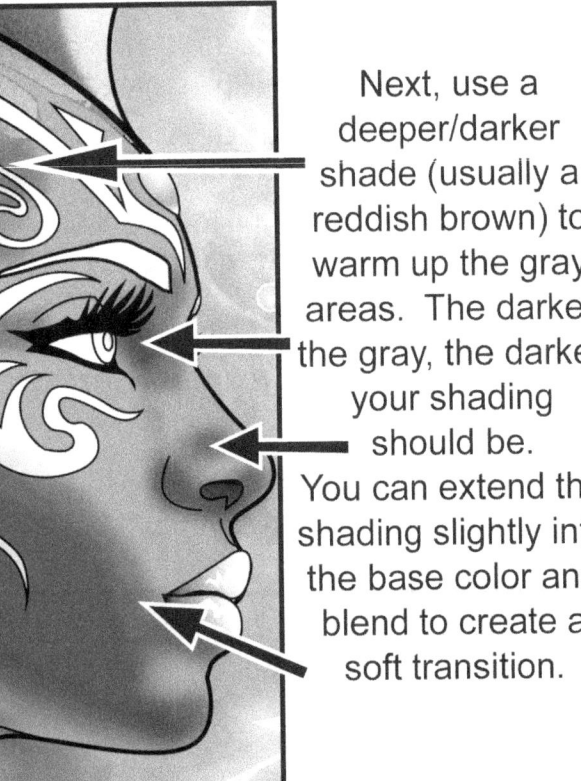

Next, use a deeper/darker shade (usually a reddish brown) to warm up the gray areas. The darker the gray, the darker your shading should be. You can extend the shading slightly into the base color and blend to create a soft transition.

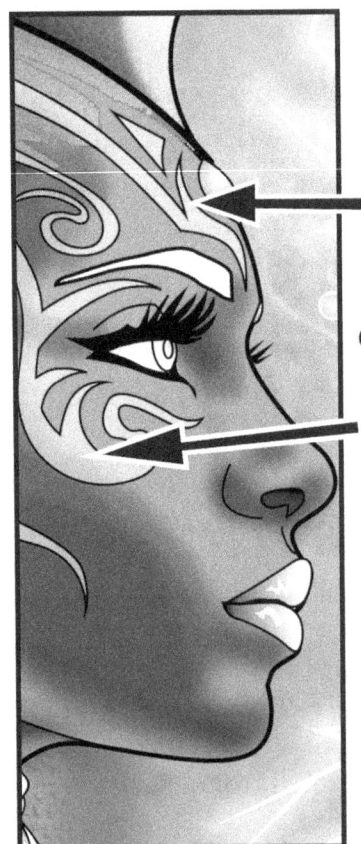

Use the same method to color the facepaint. Fill in with a transparent base color, coloring over the gray areas as well as the white areas.

(Continued on next page)

Coloring Tips

How to Use Grayscale Areas to Create Dimension (cont.)

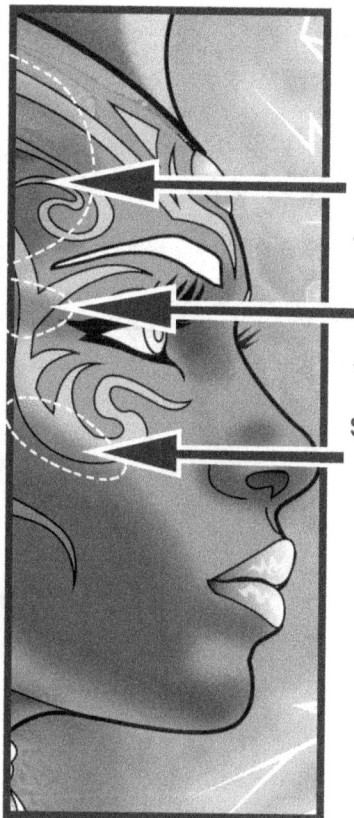

Next, use a deeper/darker shade of your base color in the gray areas. The darker the gray, the darker your shading should be. You can extend the shading slightly into the base color and blend to create a soft transition.

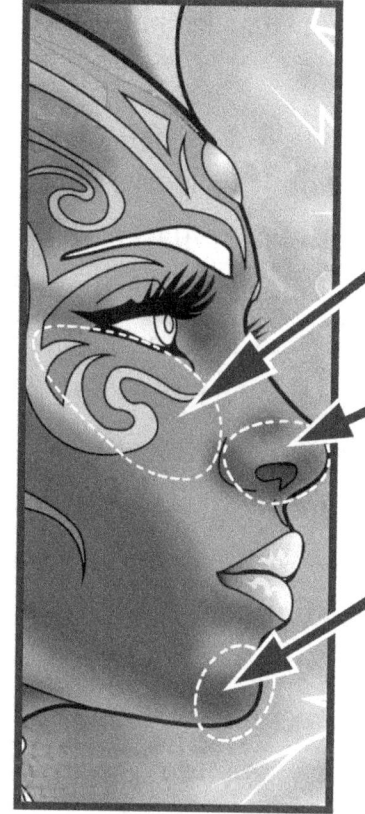

To add a little warmth and life to your skintone, use a **very light touch** with a rosey pink color on the cheeks, tip of the nose and chin areas.

Visit: www.patreon.com/CristinaMcAllister to find video tutorials and full-color images of these pages.

How to Color Luscious Lips

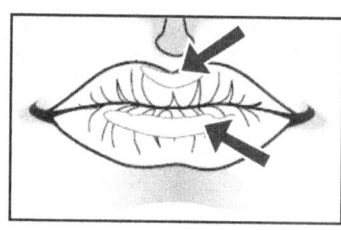

Highlight Areas

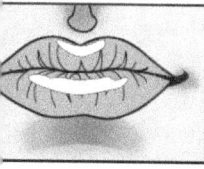

White Highlights = High Gloss look

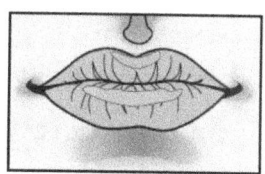

Highlights Same Color as Lips = Matte Finish look

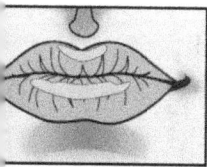

Highlights Slightly Lighter than Lip Color = Satin Finish look

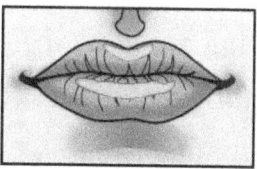

Shade undersides of lips with a deeper/darker shade to add dimension

Coloring Tips

Pages are one-sided to minimize bleed-through to the next image. If you're using markers, I recommend slipping a piece of cardstock or a few sheets of paper behind the page you're working on to make sure the ink doesn't mar the page below.

You can use a copier or scanner to print out additional copies of the pages if you want to color them again (this works best on a laser printer). Try different kinds of papers and cardstocks to see what works best for you. You can also use a paint program to colorize scanned images digitally.

Please note that you are granted permission to print out additional copies for your own personal coloring use only, not to distribute to others in any way, or to use for any commercial purpose.

You can also purchase a ready-to-print, downloadable digital edition of this book from my website:

www.gypsymystery.com/coloringbooks

Visit :www.patreon.com/Cristina McAllister
to find FREE full-color video tutorials and demos, color palette inspiration, coloring showcases, time-lapse art creation videos and more!

Use a scrap "Scribble Sheet" to test out colors and color combinations before committing them to your page. The best way to get to know your colors and how they behave is by testing and experimenting. Scribble some swatches of your colors on a scrap paper before using them to see how they look and go with the other colors of your palette.

Scribble some swatches on the **Grayscale Test Sheets** at the back of this book to see how your colors look over gray areas.

Tonal Contrast: Pay attention to the values of your colors – how light or dark they are. Adjacent areas that are similar in value will tend to harmonize visually. Adjacent areas with very different values (ex: light next to dark) will stand out and "pop". Skillful use of color value can make the difference between a flat result and a vibrant, balanced finished piece.

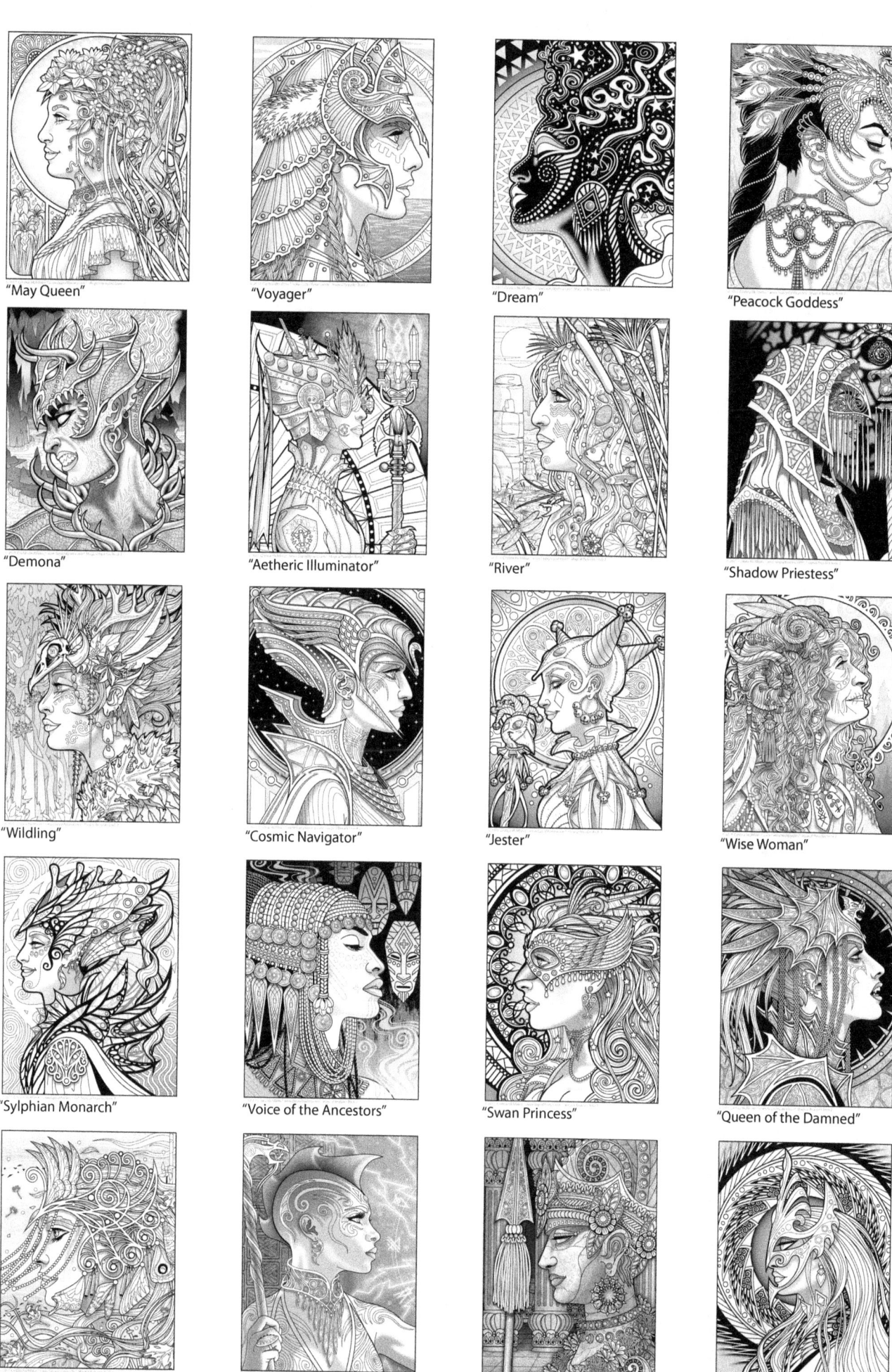

"May Queen"

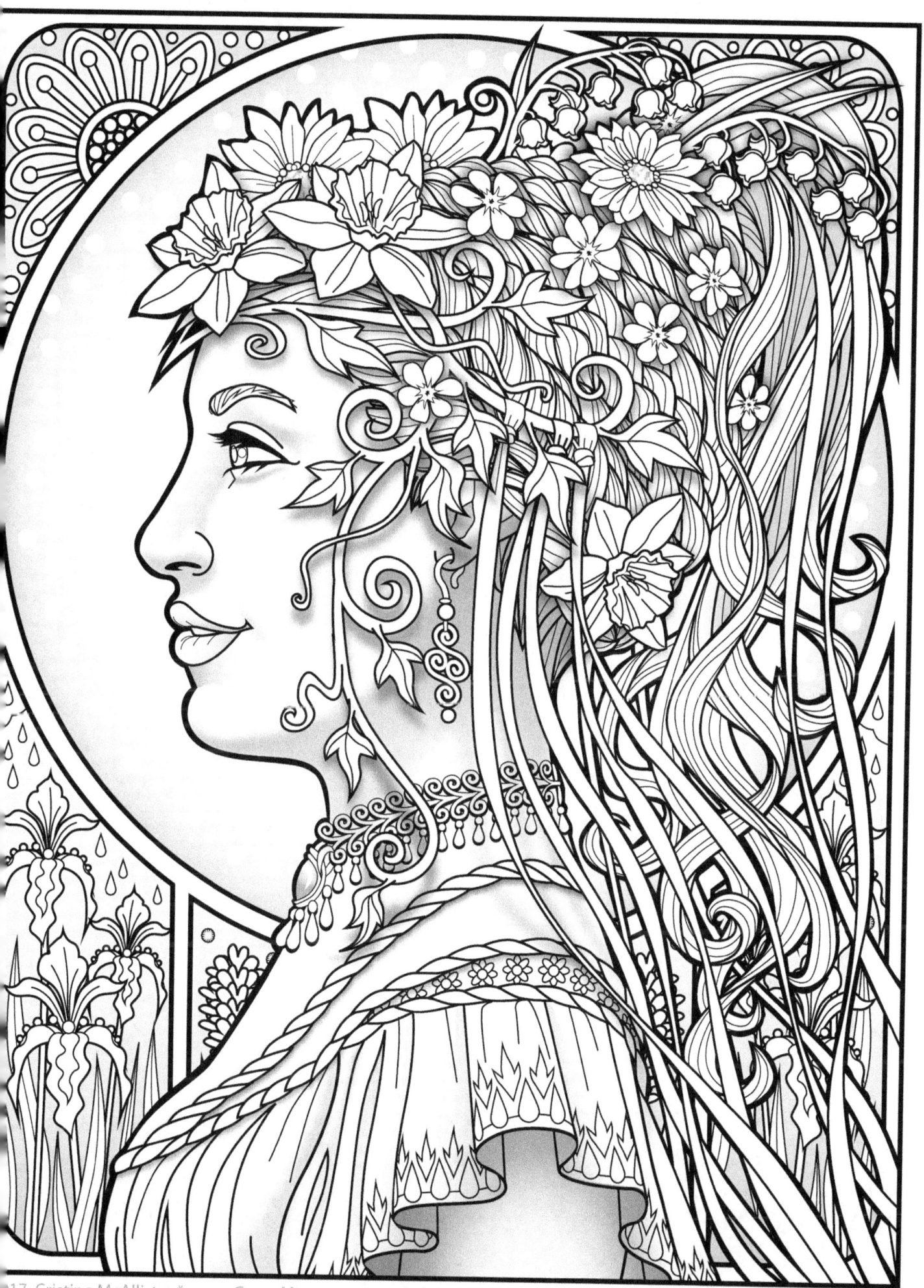

"VOYAGER"

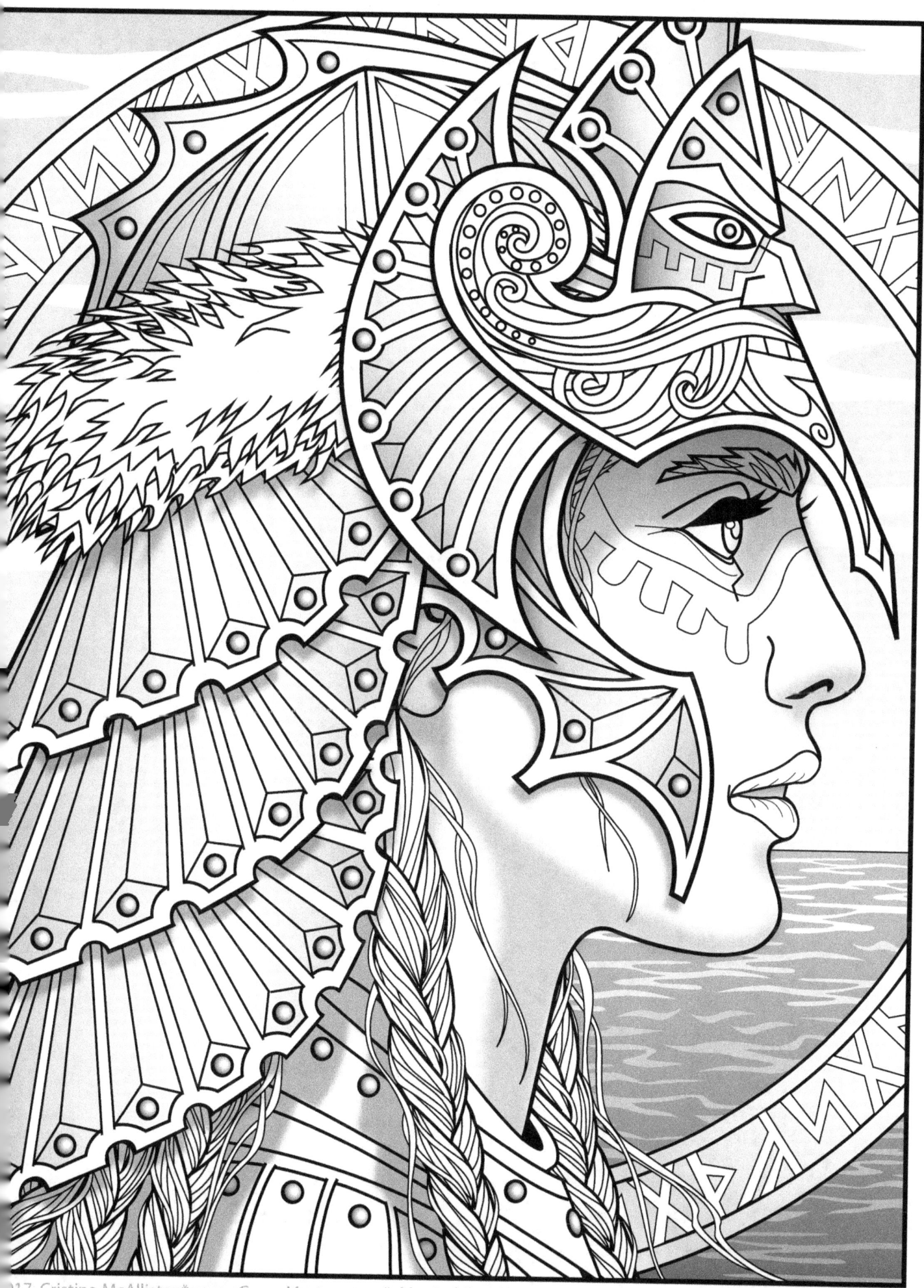

"Dream"

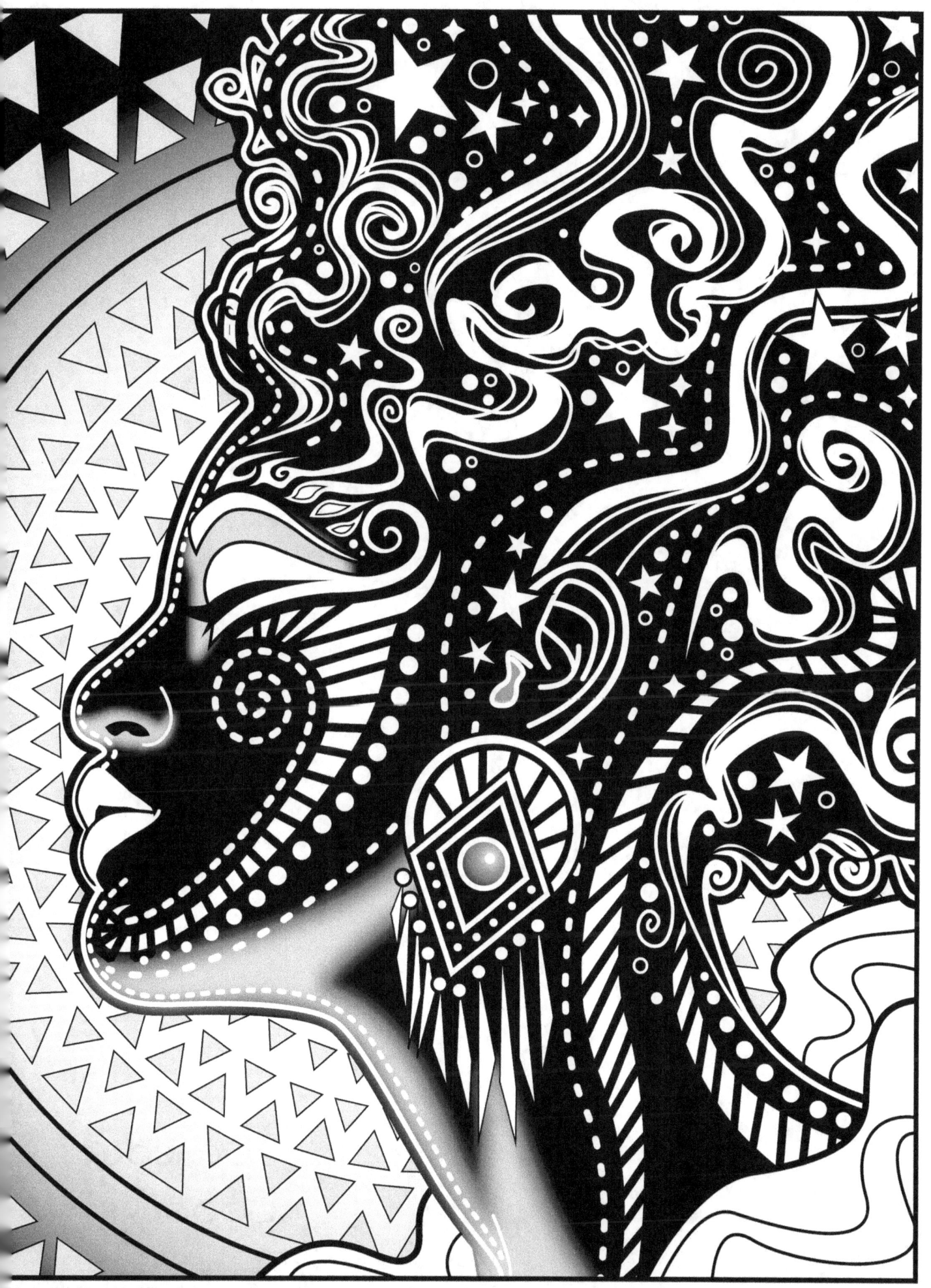

"Peacock Goddess"

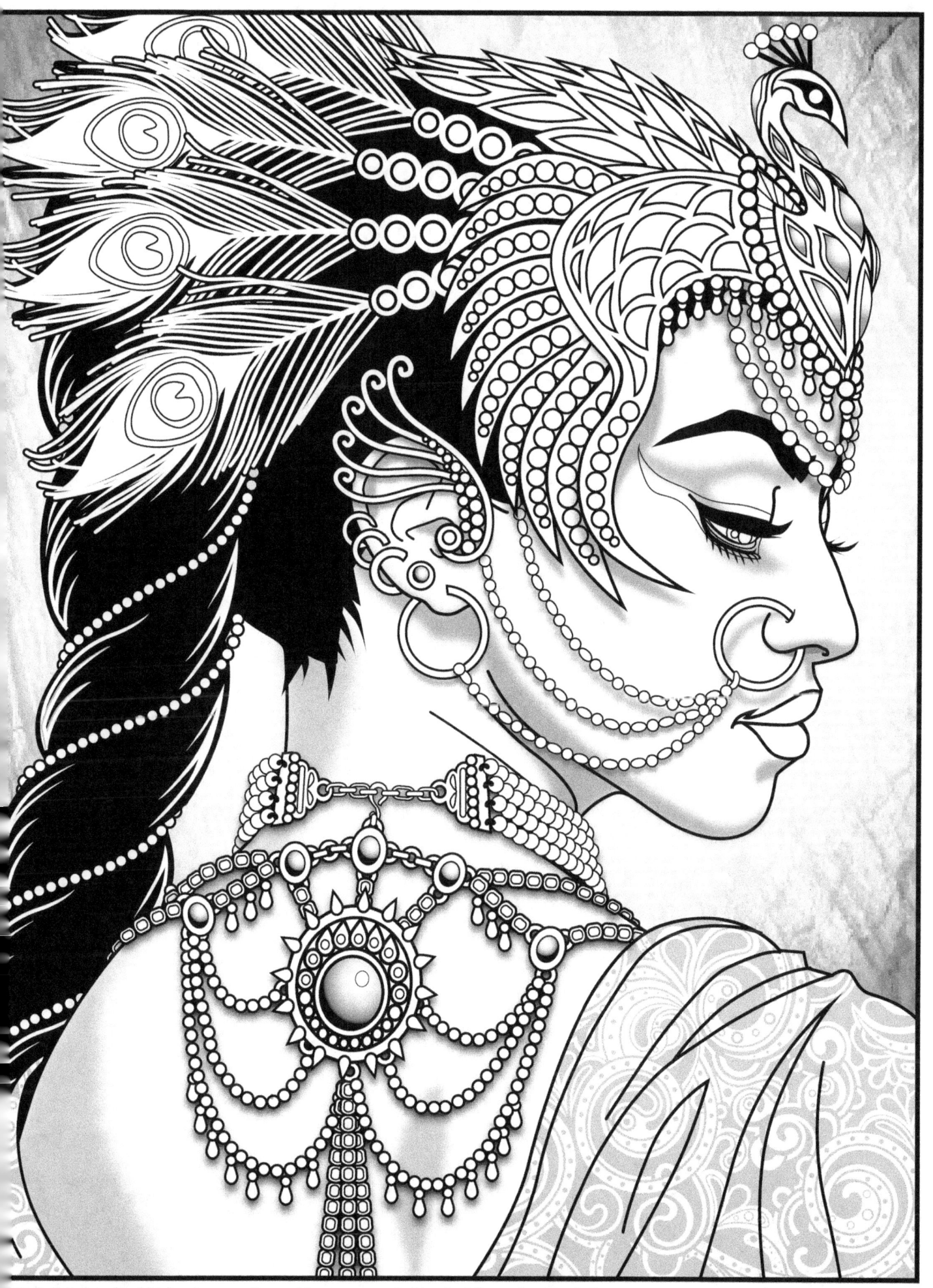

"DEMONA"

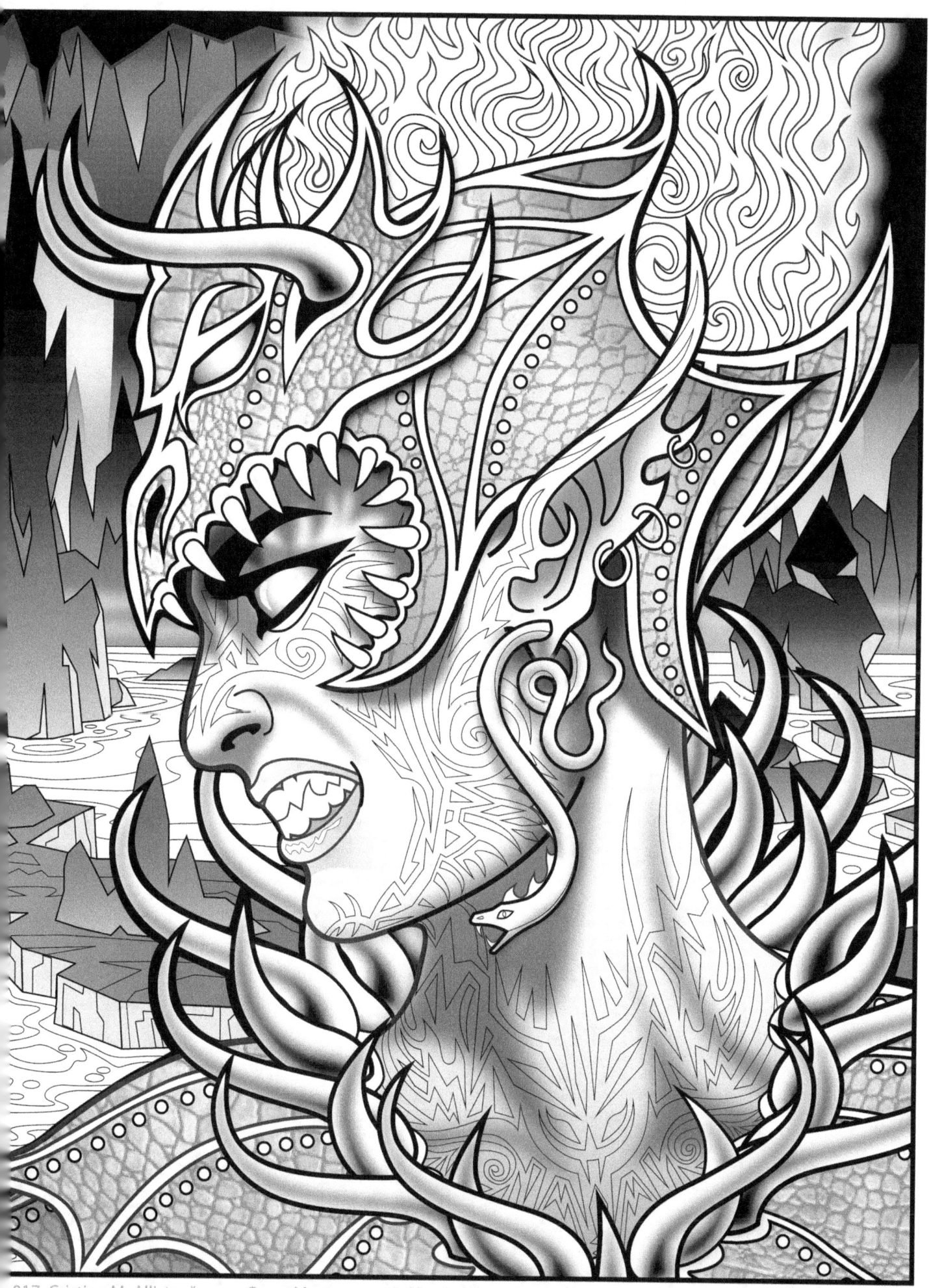

"Aetheric Illuminator"

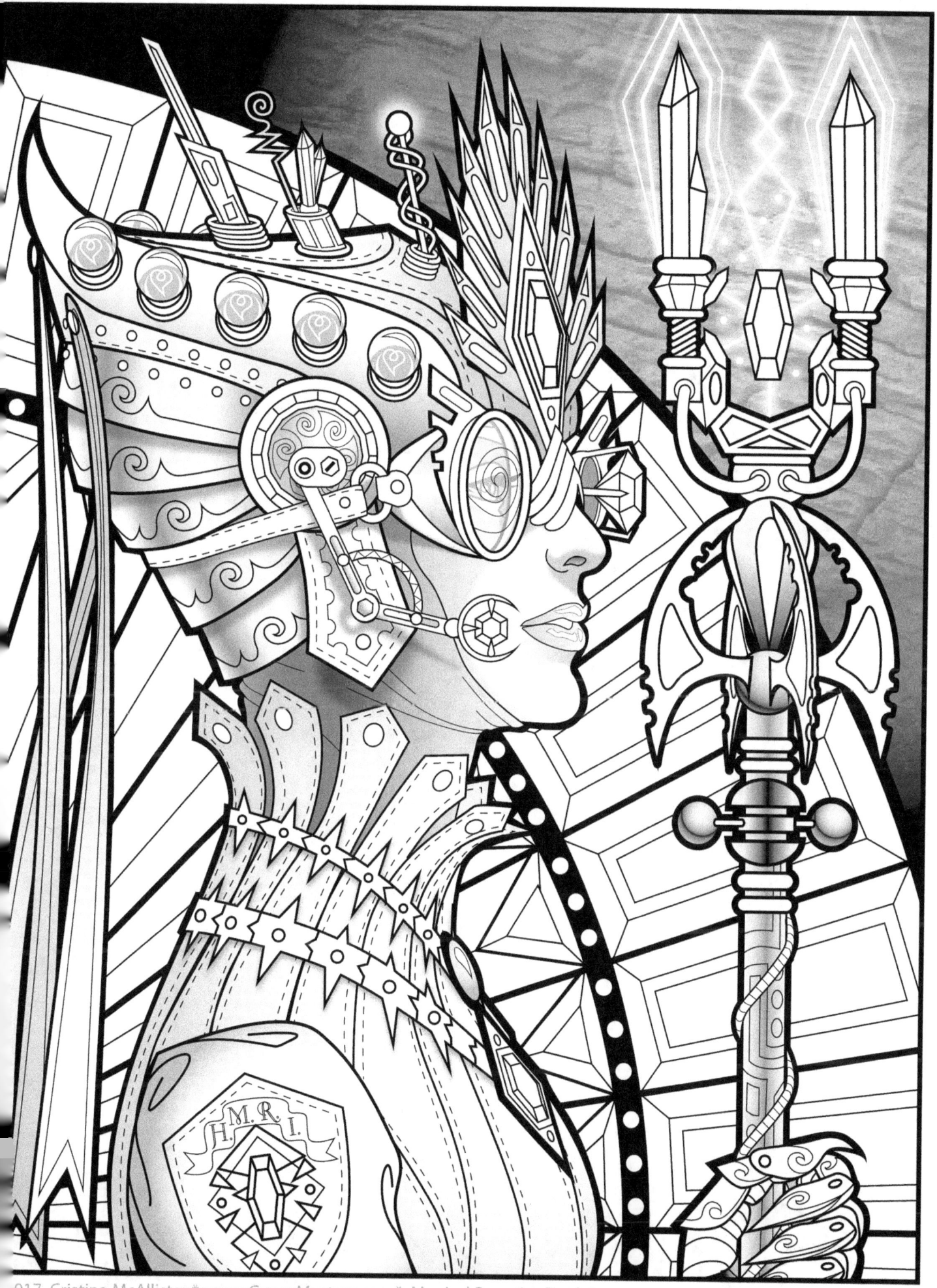

"RIVER"

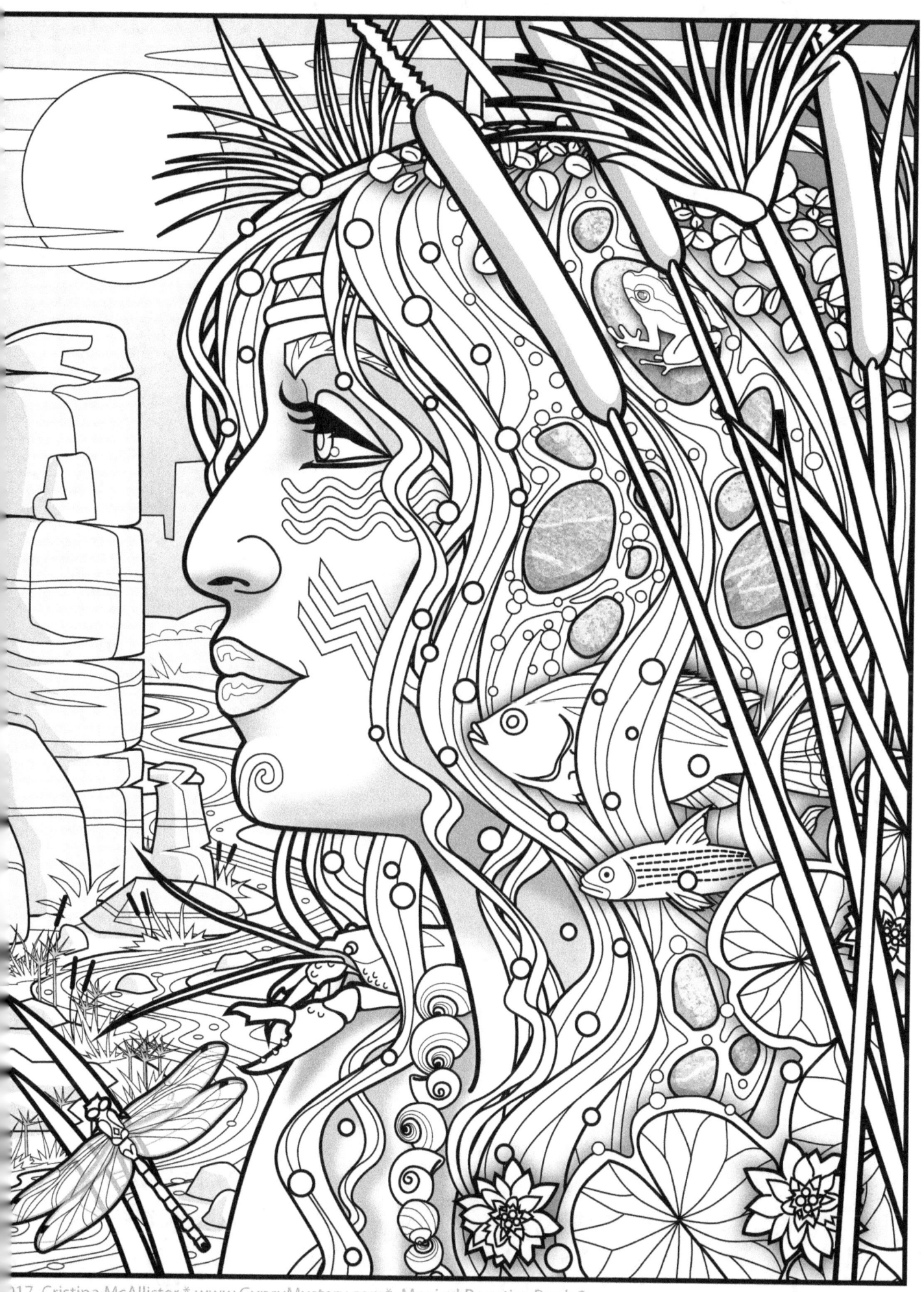

"SHADOW PRIESTESS"

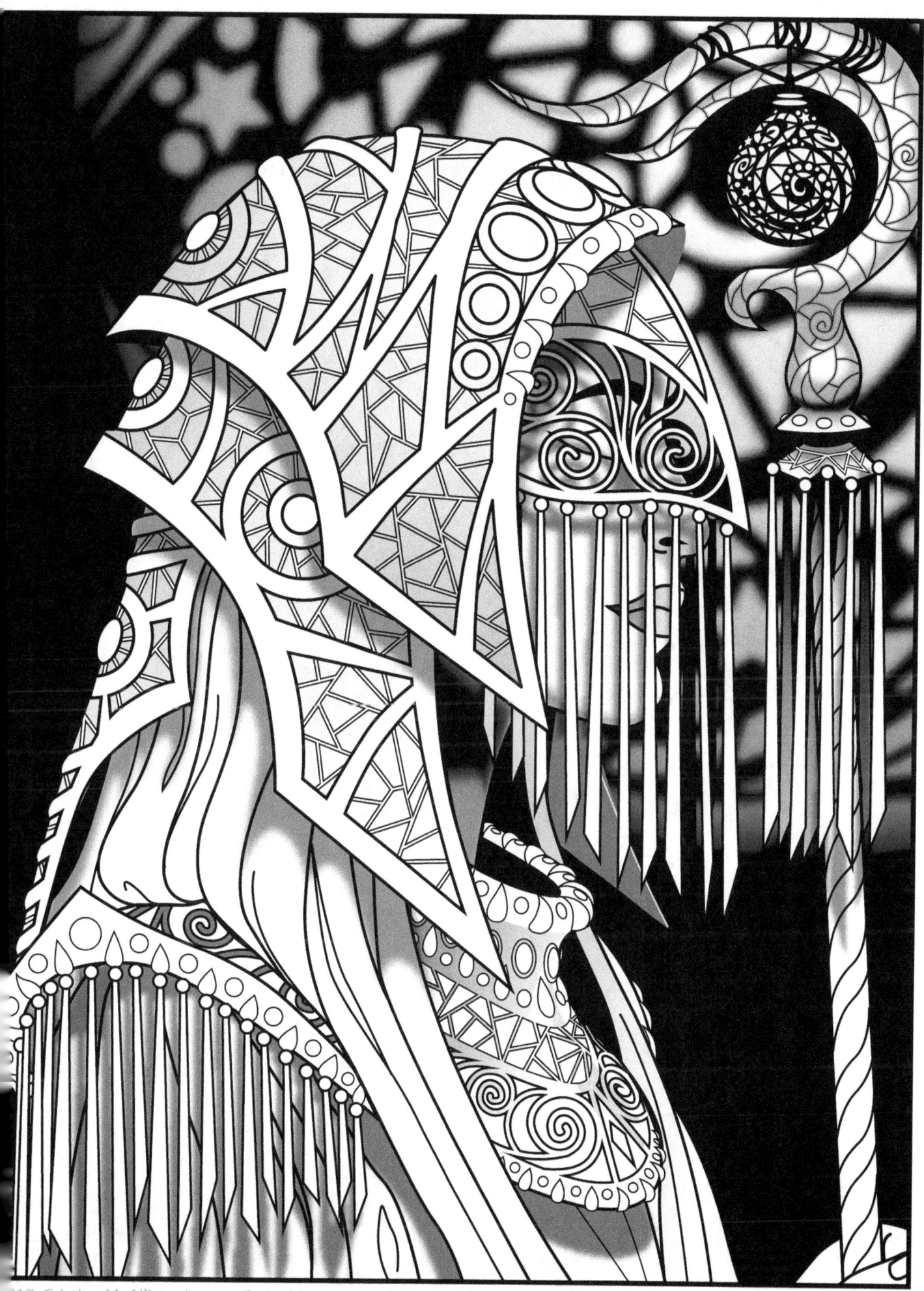

"WILDLING"

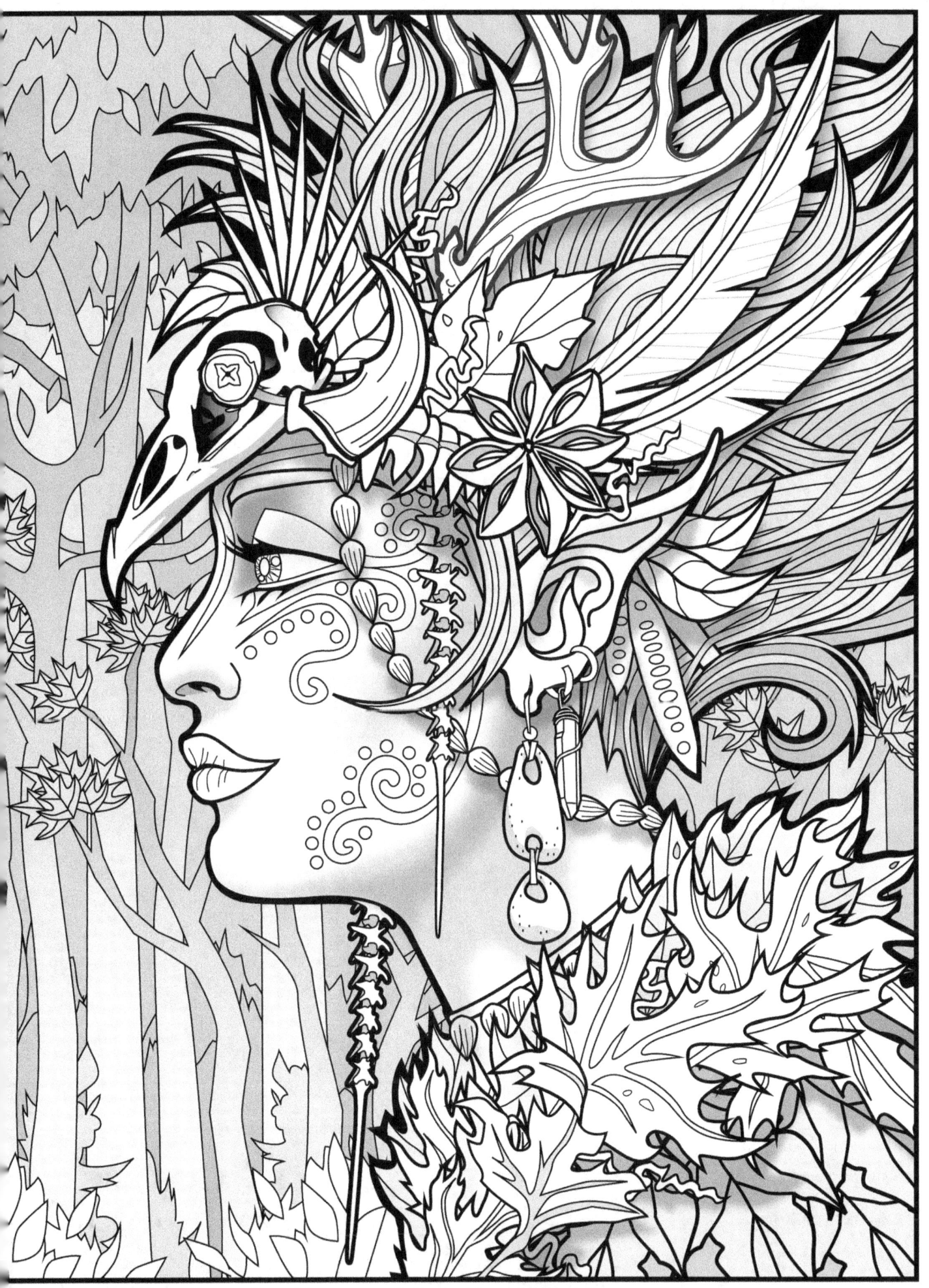

"COSMIC NAVIGATOR"

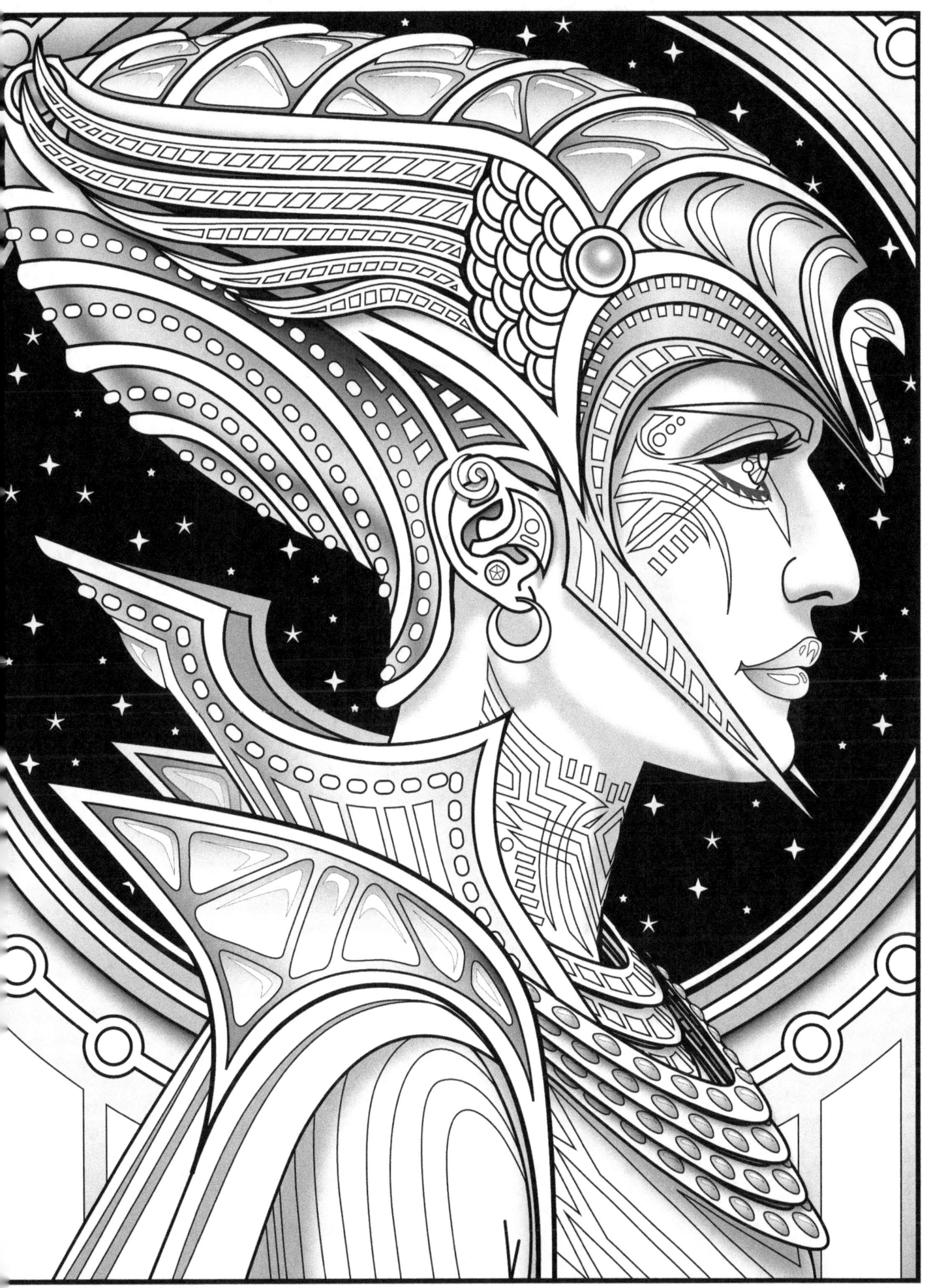

"JESTER"

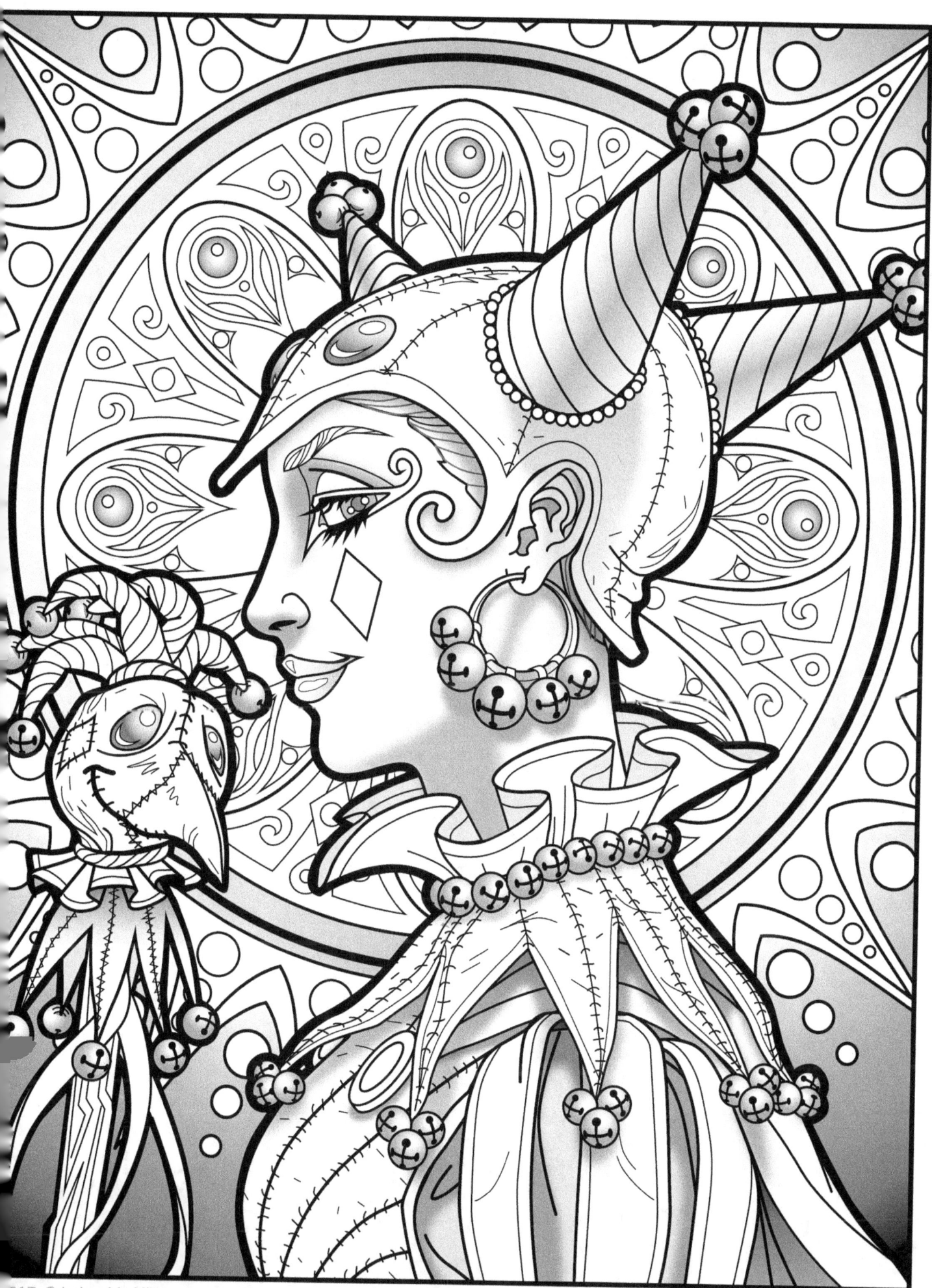

"WISE WOMAN"

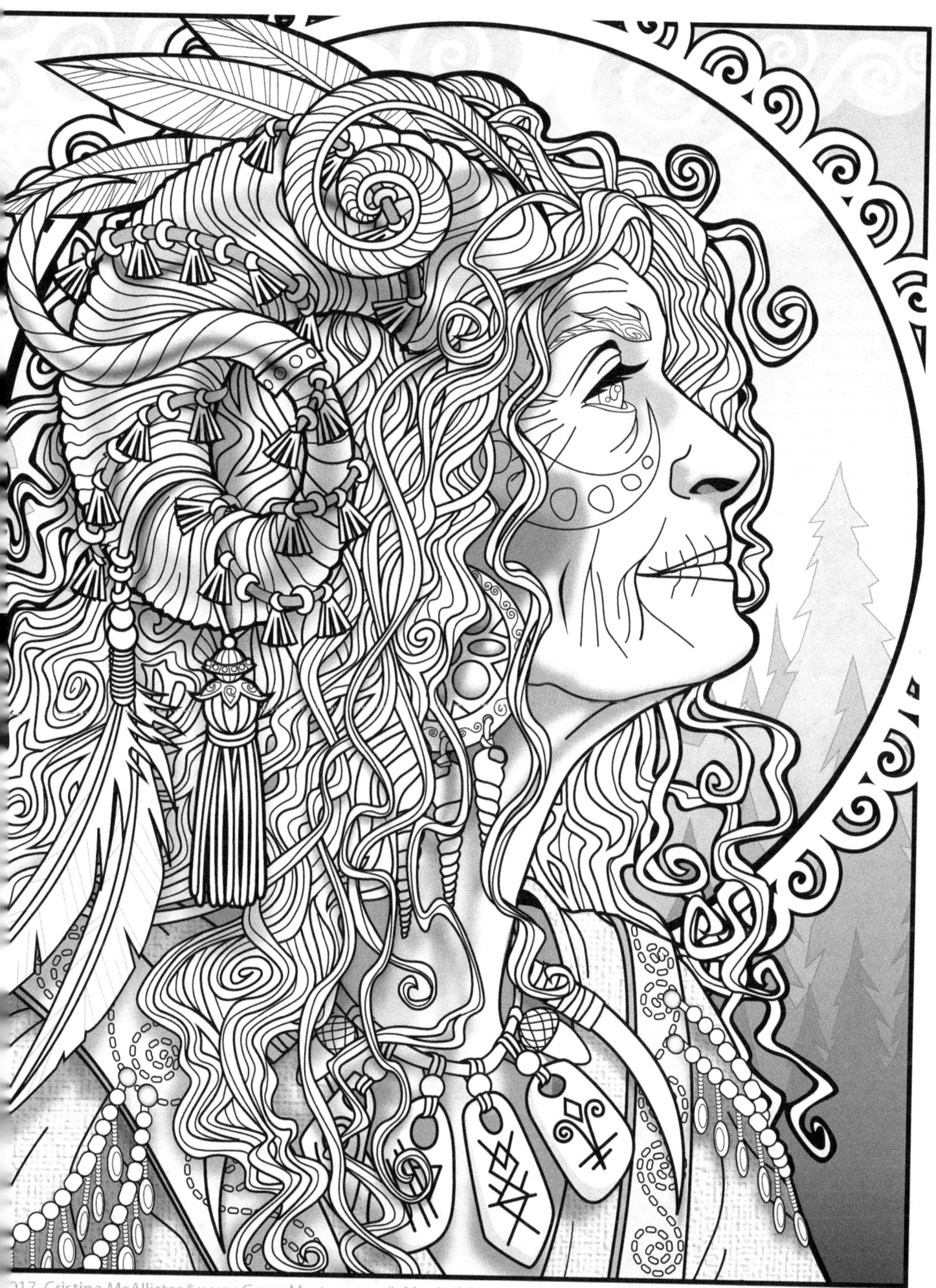

"Sylphian Monarch"

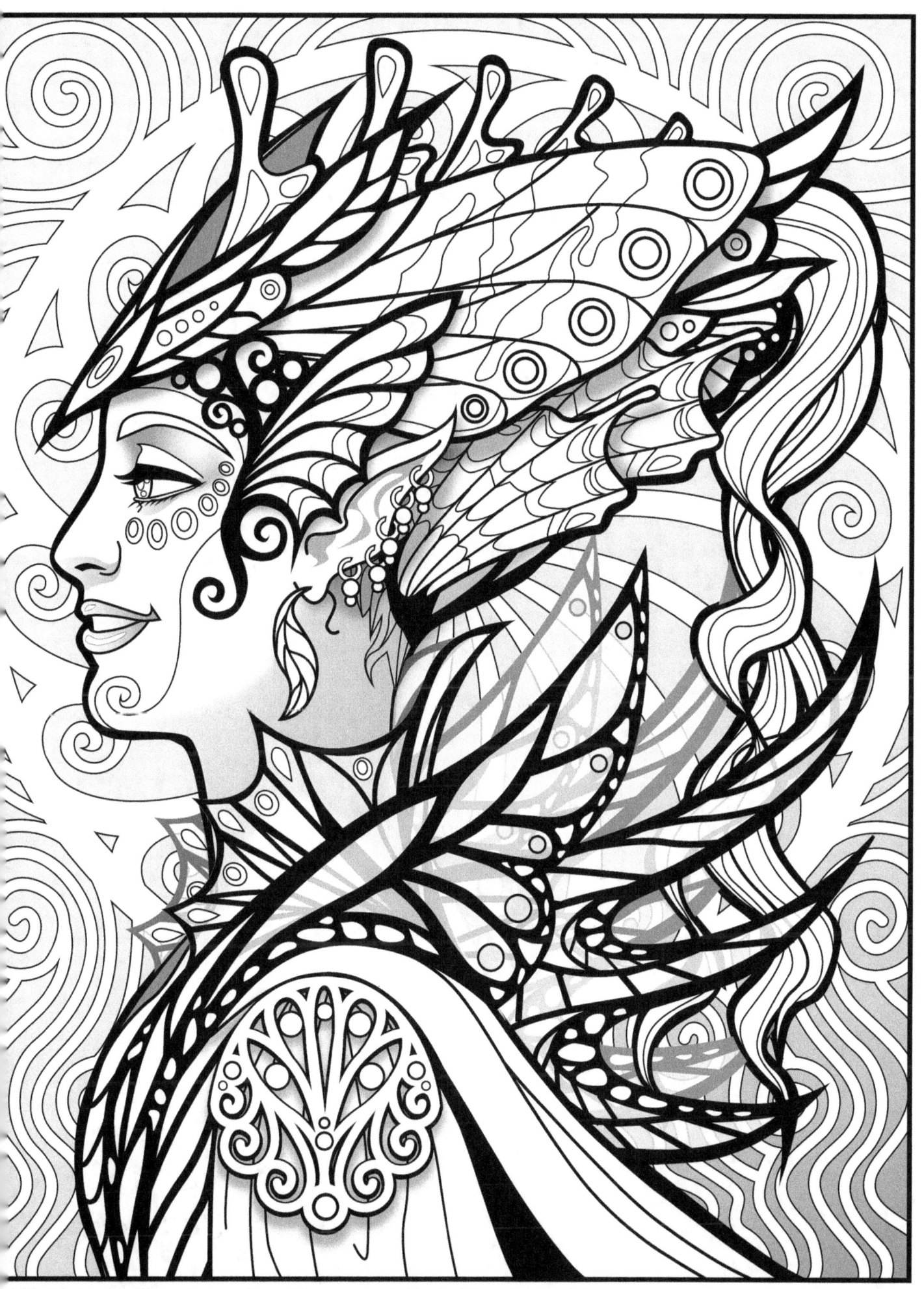

"VOICE OF THE ANCESTORS"

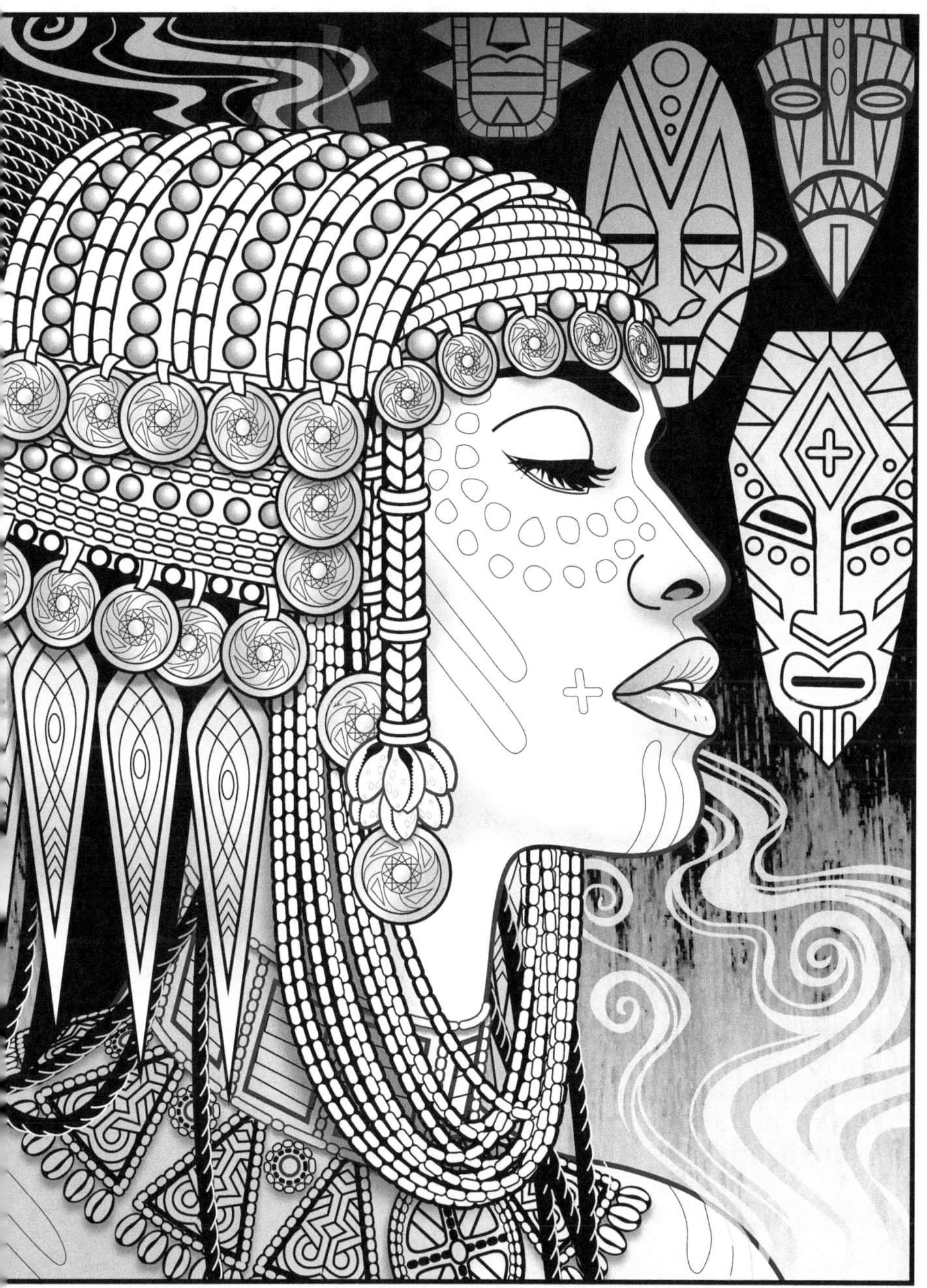

"Swan Princess"

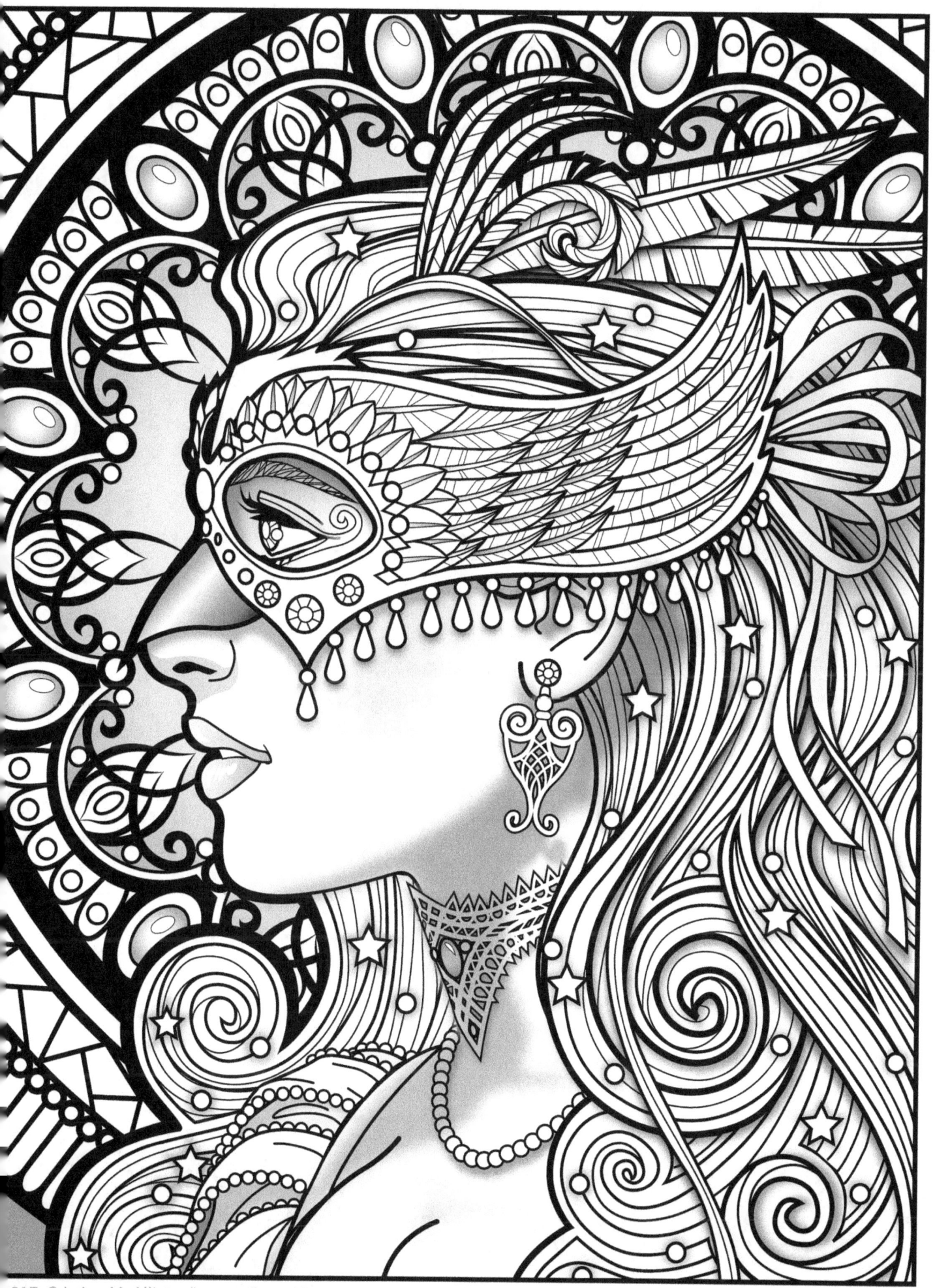

"Queen of
the Damned"

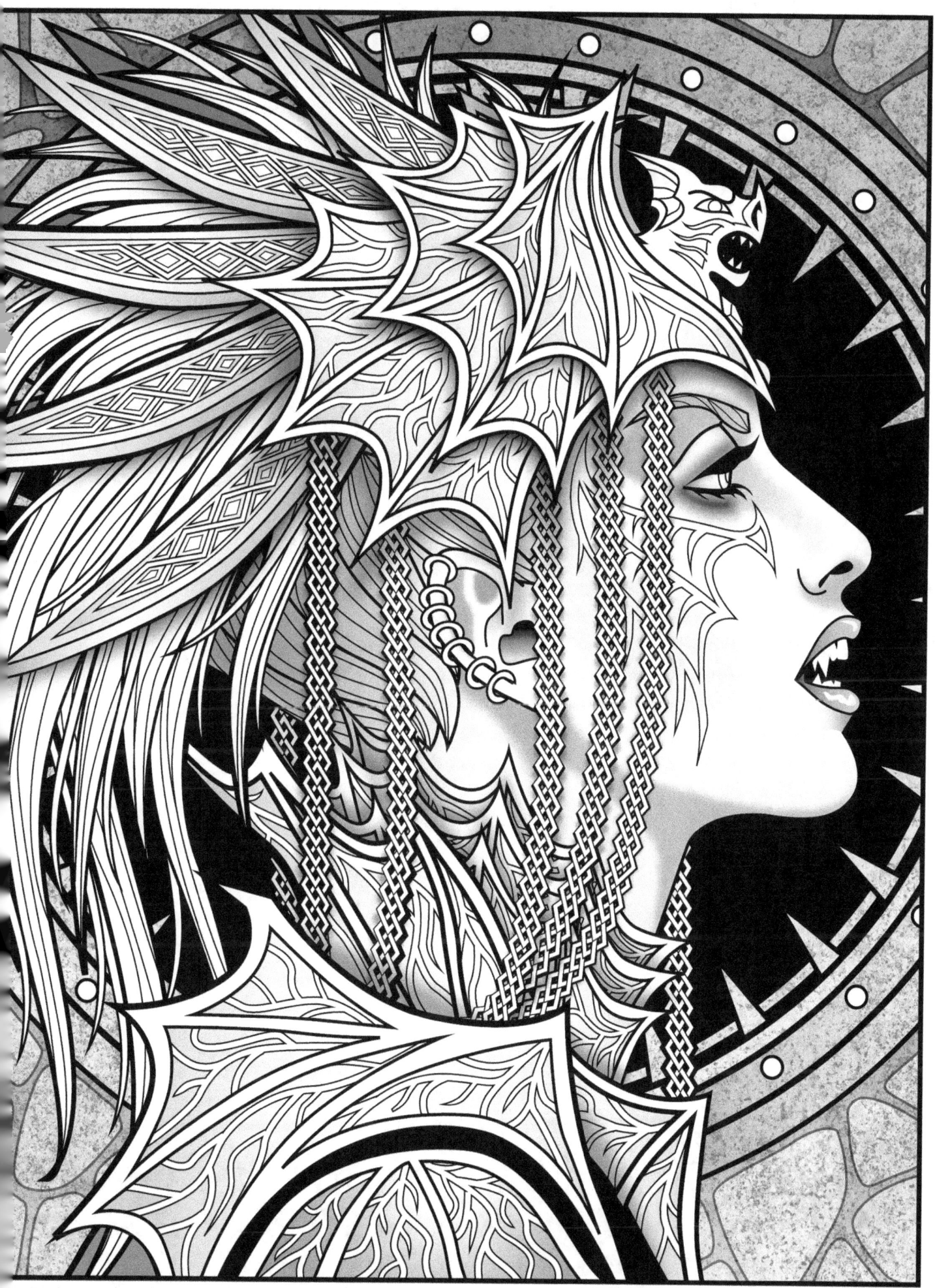

"Zephyr"

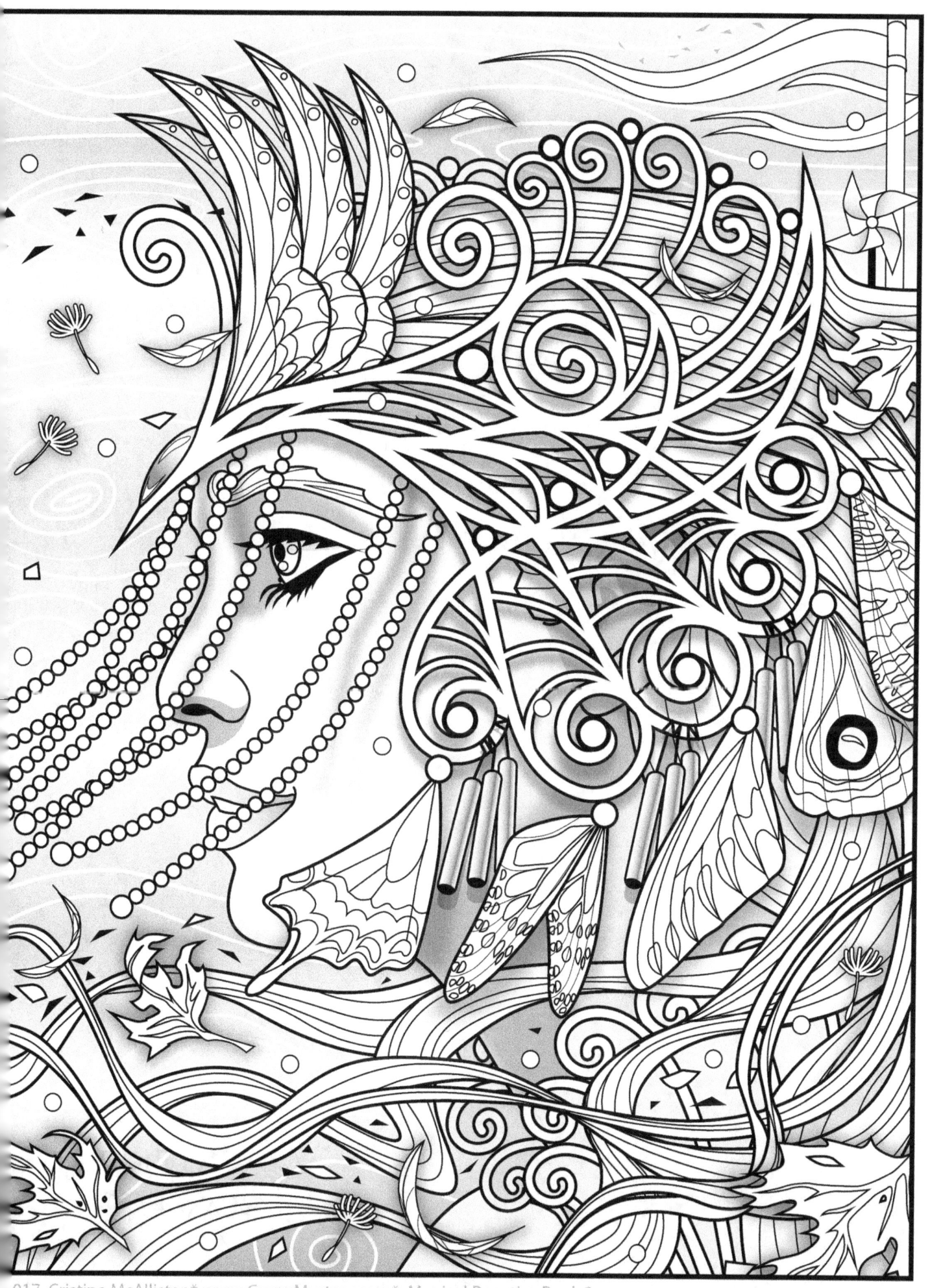

"Magnificent
Maven"

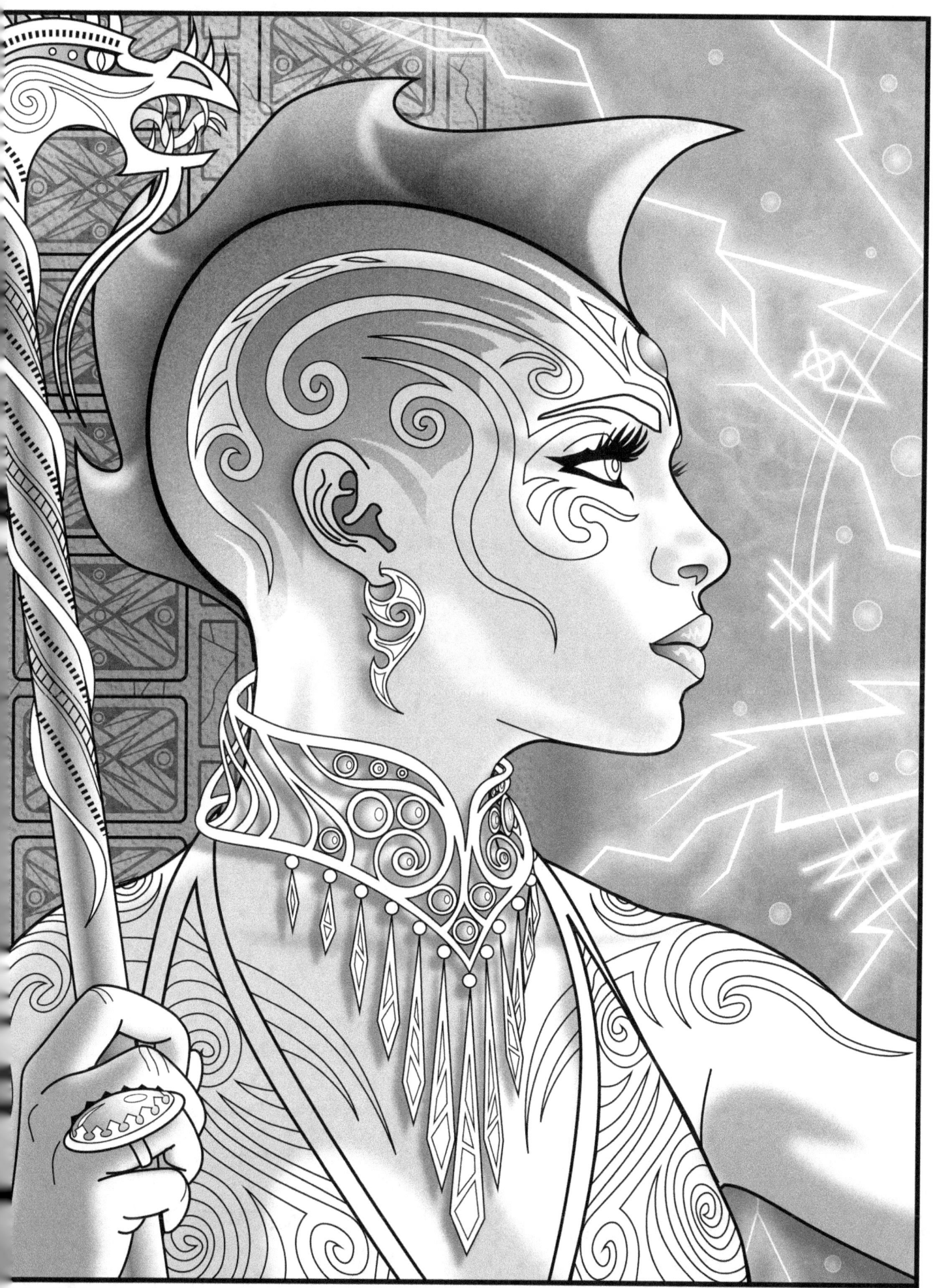

"Temple Guardian"

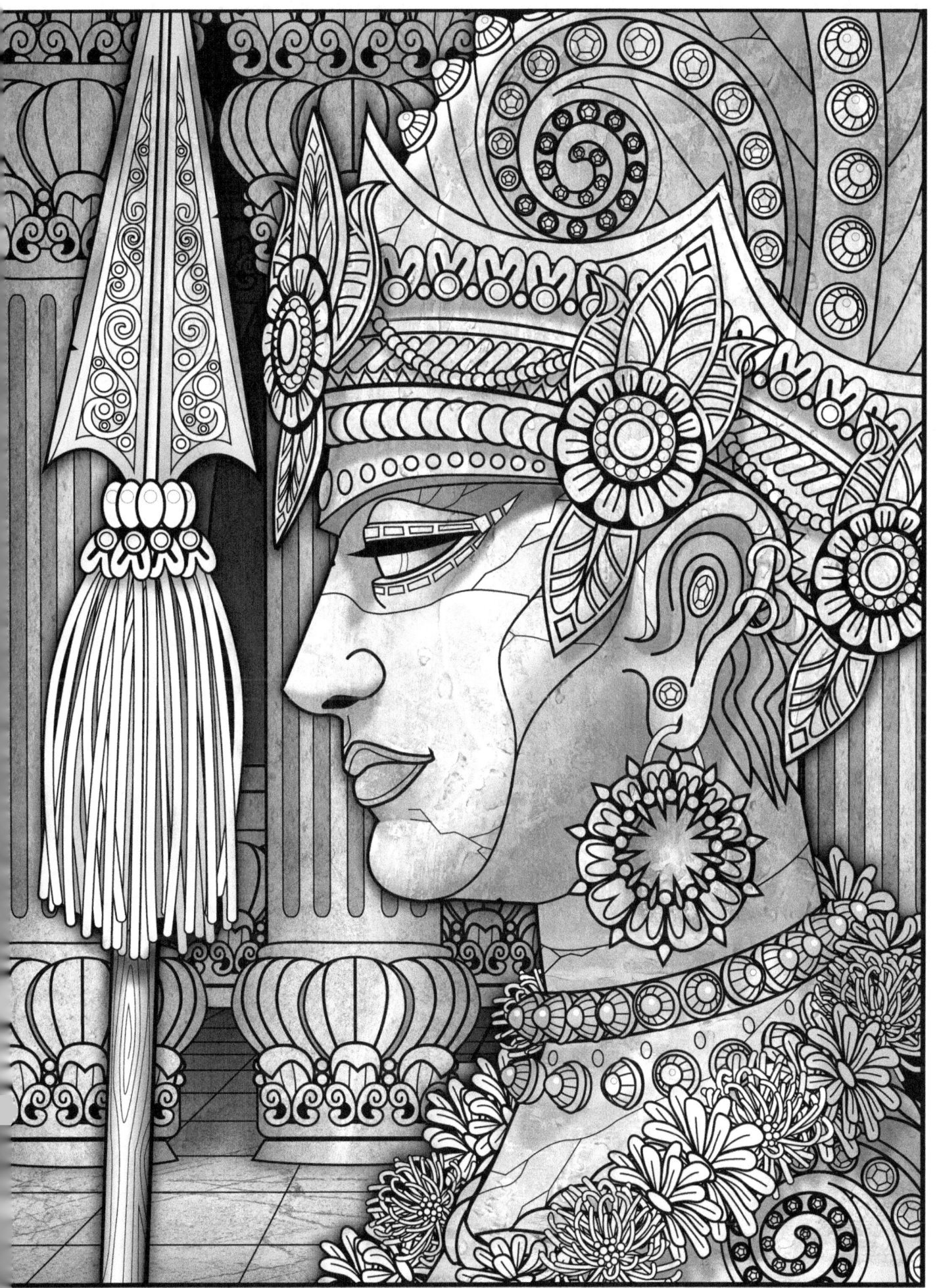

"Phoenix Commander"

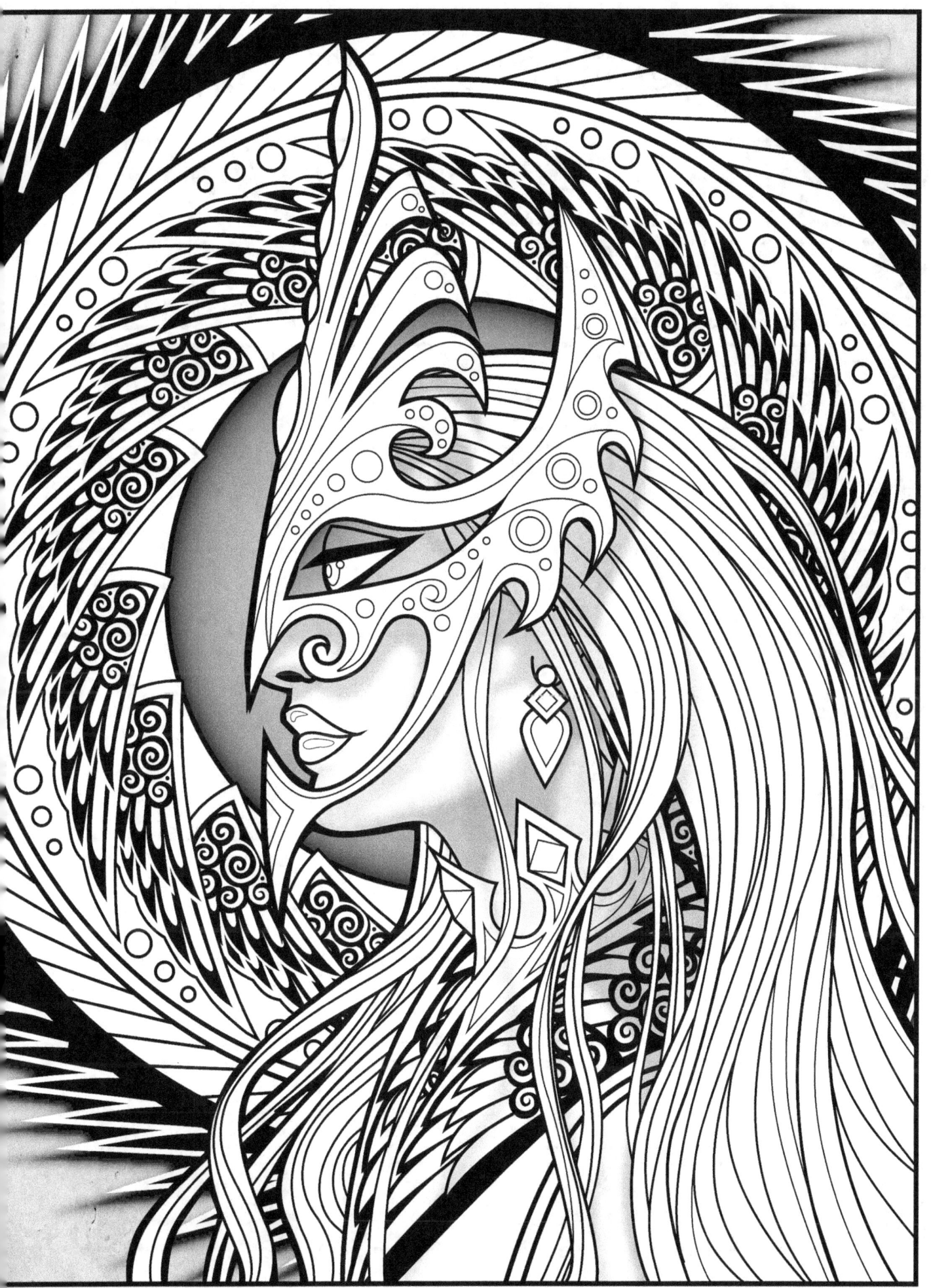

Grayscale Testing Sheet

Scribble some swatches to see how your colors work over the gray areas.

Grayscale Testing Sheet

Scribble some swatches to see how your colors work over the gray areas.

There's More to Explore at
www.GypsyMystery.com

☆ Check out more of Cristina McAllister's artwork

☆ See colored samples from this book and her other coloring books in the Coloring Page Gallery

☆ Download Print Packs and Digital Editions

Join the Cristina McAllister Coloring Club

on Facebook to see and share your WIPs and colored pages, get *exclusive FREE coloring page downloads* and MORE!

Visit: WWW.PATREON.COM/CRISTINA MCALLISTER

to find FREE video coloring tutorials and lessons, color palette ideas, time-lapse videos of the creation of the artwork for this book and video tours of all of Cristina's books.

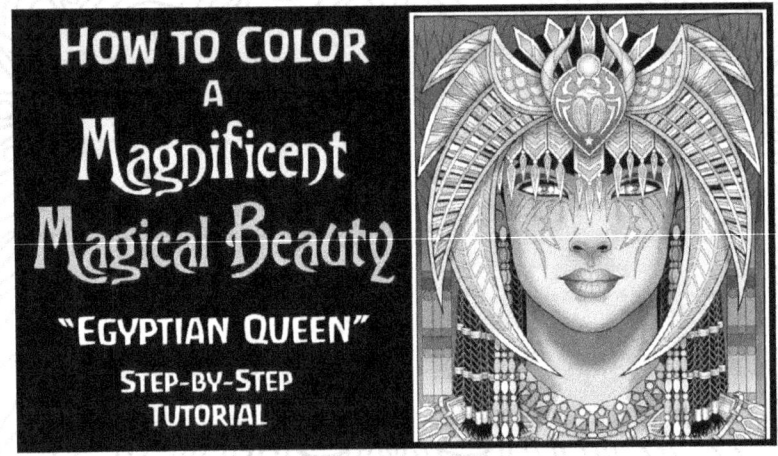

If you enjoyed this book, please don't forget to post a review on the Amazon.com listing page for the book. Even if you just leave a Star Rating, it will help other colorists find the book and decide if it's right for them.

Thanks for coloring with me!
♥ *Cristina McAllister*

www.ingramcontent.com/pod-product-compliance
Lightning Source LLC
Chambersburg PA
CBHW062203220526
45470CB00009B/2904